Beyond Bethlehem

Discovering the Boyhood of Jesus

From the Bible-Teaching Ministry of
STEPHEN DAVEY

Beyond Bethlehem

Author: Stephen Davey
Editor: Lalanne Barber
Cover Design: Paul Franitza
Body Layout: Grace Gourley
Photo of Stephen: Sam Gray Portraits, Raleigh, NC (samgrayportraits.com)
ISBN 978 0 9776641 8 4

© 2012 Stephen Davey. All rights reserved.

Unless otherwise noted, all Scripture quotations are from the New American Standard Bible®.
Copyright © 1960, 1962, 1963, 1968, 1971, 1972, 1973, 1975, 1995 by the Lockman Foundation. Used by permission.

Consideration has been made to footnote sources whenever necessary. In the case of any unintentional omission, future editions will include appropriate notations.

Contents

The Presentation of the Lamb 5

Israel's Most Wanted 27

Missing! 51

Parenting the Perfect Child 71

The Presentation of the Lamb

Luke 2:21-35

If you were to ask the average Christian today what happened to Joseph, Mary, and Jesus after the shepherds left the manger scene in Bethlehem, many would admit they don't know, while others would silently wonder if it mattered.

Besides, we've sat through enough Christmas pageants to become somewhat convinced that all the good stuff wraps up just about the time the shepherds return to their flocks, glorifying and praising God for all they had heard and seen *(Luke 2:20)*.

But what happened *next*?

Part of the challenge we face in discovering the answer is that God the Father evidently didn't want all that much recorded about His Son's early years—those between that manger scene and the commencement of His ministry thirty years later.

In His wisdom, God knew that the incarnation alone would be pretty impossible to comprehend. God as a baby was mystery enough, but God as an eight-year-old boy or a sixteen-year-old teenager would only add to the mystique and further tax the limits of our understanding.

The Lord also knew that the obscurity of His life on earth could—and would—lead to mysticism, mythology, and a host of terrible misinterpretations. Perhaps for those reasons, the record of Scripture is virtually silent.

But the Church hasn't been so quiet about it.

The early Church tried to fill in the blanks and lend a hand to the puzzle during the third and fourth centuries by creating a host of apocryphal books. Apocryphal means *hidden*, and it came to mean dubious or spurious writings by supposed church scholars.

These scholars did nothing more than catalogue legends and myths that bolstered the growing Church traditions regarding non-biblical subjects: praying to saints; the person and role of Mary; sacraments; the existence of purgatory, to name a few.

These uninspired books did more damage than good.

One particular apocryphal book called the Gospel of Thomas attempted to fill in the gaps about the boyhood of Jesus and ended up painting a portrait of Him that would have made Him as sinful a boy as any other child in need of saving.

One event recorded in this pseudo gospel has young Jesus fashioning little sparrows out of mud on the Sabbath day—which would have been considered an act of work on the Sabbath. Some children ran to tattle on Jesus but, just as Joseph arrived to punish Him for violating the Sabbath, Jesus breathed on the little dirt sparrows and they came to life and flew away, leaving behind no evidence that He had broken the Sabbath law.

Clever little boy . . . He could hide His sin just as well as any other.

On another occasion, the Gospel of Thomas records that a boy from the village threw a rock at young Jesus and it hit Him on the shoulder. Jesus turned around and cursed him, which caused the boy to immediately fall down, dead.

One incident had neighborhood boys mistreating Jesus as He played in the rain by Himself, making little puddles of water that He miraculously made clear and drinkable.

A boy came over and stomped around in Jesus' puddle, causing the water to drain away. Jesus looked up and told the boy that he wouldn't live to see the next day and, with that, the bully died.

When I was a little boy, I would love to have been able to handle bullies just as quickly as that! How great it would have been to have had supernatural power to toast the neighborhood brats—maybe not put them to death but, at least, make them break out in hives—something that would make them itch for weeks.

We had a bully in our neighborhood. You risked your life to ride your bike past his house. My ten-year-old friends and I were outside with our bikes when we noticed him walking down the street away from us. I mustered all the courage I could and pedaled my little bike safely past him (never mind that I made a few references to his family lineage as I rode past).

Only after calling him a bunch of names did I realize that I had steered my bicycle into a cul-de-sac. I was not a very bright sinner. He caught me, knocked me off my bike, and proceeded to pay me back far more than I deserved.

Keep in mind this little incident occurred *before* I was called into the ministry. But, oh, to have the power of young Jesus! Who among us would refuse the urge to settle old scores and always come out on top, whether we deserved to or not.

According to the Gospel of Thomas, Jesus' control over people extended to His own parents. On one occasion, young Jesus became upset with His stepfather Joseph and pinched his ears until they hurt, then said to him, "That is what you deserve."

When Jesus was eight years old, Thomas's Gospel records that He was helping Joseph cut wood for a bed frame. Joseph cut one of the boards too short, which was a costly mistake for this poor carpenter. Young Jesus told Joseph to pull on one end of the board while He pulled on the other—the board miraculously stretched out to the perfect length.[1]

The problems with these apocryphal, uninspired writings—and there are many—are that they describe a different Jesus. He becomes a rude, unkind, vengeful, self-centered, rebellious boy who uses His powers to fix problems that make life difficult, keeps His parents in line, and even gets rid of kids in the neighborhood who ticked Him off.

Man's attempts to fill in the blanks only sully His character and dirty His hands with a host of crimes and a menagerie of sins.

The inspired record of Scripture is vastly different.

Scriptural Confirmation

Jesus will live a life we can only imagine—a life of restraint and purity, free from any act or thought of sin—and will not use His powers to better Himself or cut down His enemies:

- From childhood, He never sinned *(Hebrews 9:14)*.
- From childhood, He perfectly fulfilled the law *(Matthew 5:17)*.

Why would this matter? It was so He could qualify as the perfect atoning Lamb, sacrificed for the sins of the whole world *(1 John 2:2)*.

When the time comes for Him to offer Himself as the blameless, sinless Lamb of God slain for our sins, He will be ready and unblemished. Not one sin will have been registered to His personal account of life.

So, as we fill in the blanks regarding Jesus' early years, let's make sure we go back to *sola scriptura* . . . what the *Scriptures* alone say.

What has the Bible revealed about the boyhood of Jesus? The Bible is not as silent as the average Christmas play might lead you to believe. It *wasn't* over after the shepherds left the manger scene. It was just beginning.

Ceremonial Confirmation

Eight days after the manger scene, some wonderful events began to unfold in the life of our infant Messiah.

Luke's inspired account provides the information:

> ***And when eight days had passed, before His circumcision, His name was then called Jesus, the name given by the angel before He was conceived in the womb*** (Luke 2:21).

In this passage, Jesus and His parents are involved in three ceremonies that actually reveal so much about this couple and the home they established for Jesus.

The Ceremony of Identification

According to the prescribed Old Testament law, every Jewish baby boy would be circumcised eight days after

The Presentation of the Lamb

birth—that is, if the baby's parents cared at all about God's Word.

This act was commanded in ***Genesis 17***; had Jesus not been circumcised, He would not be identified with His people, even though both His parents were descendants of Abraham.

Circumcision brought a boy into the national life of the Hebrew people and identified him with Abraham's household of faith.

By faithfully fulfilling this command, Jesus will actually be eligible to fulfill the promises that God had pledged to Abraham.[2]

So this simple act speaks volumes about the character of Joseph and Mary. They were following God's Word relating to the Abrahamic covenant, and their obedience was nothing less than a statement of personal faith.

For every faithful Jewish family, circumcision was considered so sacred a duty that it could be carried out on the Sabbath day.

A Jewish leader or doctor would perform the cutting away of the foreskin. At some point in the ceremony, the parents would announce the name of the child.

Imagine that first scene beyond Bethlehem. The painful cry of Jesus pierced the air, becoming His first moment of suffering at the hand of mankind. These were among His first tears after having taken on human flesh.

His humiliation and suffering had already begun. He became acquainted with sorrow long before the cross.

Joseph and Mary are also suffering. Already they are somewhat dazed, confused, ostracized, and alone. These two teenagers—Joseph, perhaps a little older than Mary—have traveled to Bethlehem under a cloud of suspicion. What a whirlwind it had been: nine months of turmoil mixed with trust.

It was an angel's visit that convinced Joseph to take Mary to be his wife after she was found to be pregnant during their betrothal. It would be the scandal of Joseph's family and their entire village.

There would be no wedding ceremony or wedding march. There would be no family festival where the village celebrated the union of Joseph and Mary.

Baby Jesus will add an exclamation point to their guilt... guilt that Mary and Joseph will never live down; the rumors will never go away.

In fact, when Jesus Christ makes His claim to be the Messiah, the Jewish leaders will dig up the dirty rumors again and throw back into Jesus' face the accusation:

We were not born of fornication [like You] (John 8:41).

They may as well have added, "We know how you got your start—don't lecture *us*."

Joseph and Mary will move from the stable into humble quarters somewhere in Bethlehem while Joseph will pick up odd jobs to support his young family, using his tools and his calloused hands.

With that as a backdrop, can you see their faith more clearly? Even though they will *never* be viewed by the Jewish community as credible, godly, obedient children of Abraham, they still insist on identifying their Son with the Jewish family through circumcision.

They will refuse to adjust their character to match the incorrect perception of them. They will refuse to live up to the misconception that they cared nothing for the Word of God.

Watch them carefully here as they identify Jesus with the Law of God. Ask yourself what it takes to keep you from submitting to the Word of God. False accusations? Unwarranted rumors? Unfair criticism? Malicious gossip?

- Will you obey God even when it invites ridicule?
- Will you forfeit a relationship because of your passion for holiness?
- Will you identify with the people of God even if it causes those at your job or in your family to believe that you have gone off the deep end?

What does it take for you to say, "If this is what walking by faith means, I'm gonna sit this one out? If obeying God leads to this kind of misunderstanding or accusation or

BEYOND BETHLEHEM

mistreatment, never mind. If doing the right thing causes so much discomfort, surely God will understand if I wriggle out of this one."

Don't overlook the fact that all the pain and suffering and confusion and accusation swirling around this young family has not hounded them because they missed God's will—it's *because* of God's will.

Their experiences were not the result of disobeying God but, rather, their insistence on obeying Him . . . down to the most minute detail.

It is against this backdrop of *permanent* discomfort that Joseph and Mary refuse to disobey the command of God . . . they will not miss one step.

And so, on the eighth day, as they brought forward their little Boy, they sent out quite a message: even though everyone believed Jesus was illegitimate—born of fornication—this family will identify with the people of God and the Word of God and the will of God.

It was during this ceremony of circumcision they delivered His name. Luke writes, ***His name was then called Jesus*** (Luke 2:21).

This was the name chosen for Him before time began. The angel had come to both Mary and Joseph individually to tell them: when the ceremony of identification arrives, give Him the name **Jesus** *(Matthew 1:21; Luke 1:31)*.

To understand the significance of this name, you have to travel back to the first person to have ever been given the name. He was a young man at the time when his name was changed. He had been born into Egyptian slavery, along with all the other Hebrew slaves under Pharaoh's cruel reign. This little Jewish boy had been given the name as a sheer act of faith: he was named Hoshea, which means *salvation*.

G. Campbell Morgan, the late expositor, wrote that this name was a sigh and a hope—a sob from his parents who dared, by faith, to believe in deliverance so much that they named their son Salvation.[3]

He would eventually grow up to become the assistant to Moses, and Moses would later change his name from Hoshea to Joshua.

Moses simply took letters from the great name Yahweh (Jehovah) and some letters from the boy's name Hoshea and wove them into one name so that the young man's name became Yehoshua, which means *Jehovah is salvation*.

The name was shortened to Joshua and the Greek counterpart to this Hebrew name was Yeshua. We pronounce it in English *Jesus*. It carried with it the idea that the person so named would become an agent of salvation—he could be the promised Deliverer.

Hundreds of little boys playing in the streets and villages throughout Israel were named Jesus, a father or mother hoping that, perhaps, their son would one day play a role in the deliverance of Israel.

None of them would . . . no one but this little Boy.

He was and still is *the* agent of salvation. He is both Jehovah and salvation in one.

I can't help but wonder who was at this ceremony to hear the announcement of His name.

Did the Jewish doctor stifle a yawn? Did the Rabbi standing there shake his head at the audacity of this peasant couple—two people without references or attending family members. How could they believe their Child—from all appearances, conceived in sin—would ever deliver *anybody*?

What a testimony to Christ's condescension! He had come without fanfare to His nation. The hosts of heaven couldn't keep from bursting onto the scene, but their singing had been contained on the back hills of Bethlehem. The only ones who had seen and heard the celestial choir proclaim that the Savior had indeed been born were shepherds.

Shepherds weren't permitted to serve as witnesses in any Hebrew court. No one would believe them.

But now, under the knife and into the covenant, the true Deliverer has just identified with His people . . . and they have no idea.

Afterward, Joseph and Mary and their eight-day-old Son, still whimpering in pain, slipped back to their undisclosed home in the poorer section of Bethlehem.

They had carefully met the demands of the Law. They had observed the ceremony of identification.

THE PRESENTATION OF THE LAMB

The Ceremony of Redemption

Luke continues in his writing:

> ***And when the days for their purification according to the law of Moses were completed, they brought Him up to Jerusalem to present Him to the Lord*** (Luke 2:22).

Now if you go back to **Leviticus 12**, you'll discover that the days of purification for a new mother of a male child was forty days. Following that period of waiting, she could attend with her husband and child another special ceremony before the Jewish priesthood.

The ceremony symbolized the right of God as the owner of the child. The parents would give a gift of five shekels, symbolically redeeming their son from priestly service. They effectively bought their son back from God.

The last portion of this verse explains:

> **[A]*s it is written in the Law of the Lord, "Every firstborn male that opens the womb shall be called holy to the Lord"*** (Luke 2:23).

Simply put, God had a claim to the firstborn male. They were to be holy; that means *separated unto God.*

If the male child was from the tribe of Levi, he would later serve as a priest in Israel. The priests were the government: the senators and representatives. They ran the religious and civil systems or, at least, as much as the Roman government allowed them during the days of Christ.[4]

This was, effectively, an Israeli draft for priestly service, and there were no exceptions.

But since Christ was born into the tribe of Judah, He was not required to serve in the priestly system. As a result, Joseph and Mary were able to pay what was called a *redemption tax* (**Numbers 18**: five shekels) and redeem Jesus from God. This was called the Redemption of the Firstborn.[5]

Frankly, they really had no idea of the irony of this particular redemption ceremony. Here they are, buying Jesus back from God, when Jesus had actually come *from* God to purchase a people *for* God.

They were redeeming the Redeemer!

They were exempting from priestly service the One who would serve as High Priest forever. Amazing!

And don't miss the fact that in order for Joseph and Mary to obey this ceremonial law, it would only add to their poverty. They've already paid the census tax in Bethlehem, and now they were required to fork over five shekels—an amount equivalent to several days' wages.

But again, they were willing to take whatever steps necessary to fulfill the letter of the Law, and we read of no complaint from either of them.

To Joseph and Mary, the will of God was taxing, tiring, uncomfortable, uneasy, lonely, *and* expensive.

The Presentation of the Lamb

They were God's chosen couple to bear and raise the Redeemer. But so far, God had not paid them anything but a few angelic visits . . . *they* seemed to be paying at every turn.

But to them, cost obviously was not an issue—obedience was. And they were willing to pay any price that obedience demanded.

In fact, you need to know that Joseph and Mary were not required by law to bring Jesus all the way to Jerusalem for this ceremony. They could have paid the five shekels to a local priest and saved all the wear and tear on their cart and their bodies, not to mention lost wages from missing work.

For them to show up in Jerusalem was going above and beyond.

Why would they want to go to Jerusalem's temple to present Jesus to the priest and pay the redemption tax? Luke provides a clue:

> ***They brought Him up to Jerusalem to present Him to the Lord*** (Luke 2:22*b*).

No one else knew who Jesus was—but they did. And they knew God did. They weren't just presenting Jesus to the priest; they were presenting Him to God.

And irony yet again: they were presenting the *Lord* to the *Lord*. They didn't fully understand it, and neither can we.

In their childlike faith, they came to the national center for worship:

- presenting the Savior to the Sovereign;

- dedicating God the Son to God the Father;
- presenting the Lamb of God to God;
- bringing the Lord of the Temple to the Temple of the Lord;[6]
- not thinking that the Object of true worship has just arrived at the house of worship;
- not knowing that the One who would rip down the curtain between mankind and the Holy of Holies was at this very moment cradled by a virgin girl standing yards away from the Holy of Holies.

And in all the hubbub in the temple that day, no one could have dreamed that every ritual, every sacrifice, every activity on those grounds illustrated and pointed by faith toward the longed for, coming, final sacrifice of the Baby who was in their midst.

At the very moment when prayers were ascending and incense was burning and sacrifices were offered, with hundreds of people milling around them . . . there He was!

The Lamb of God had come.

God became flesh—He came to live among us—and, as John's Gospel account records,

> [A]*s many as received Him* [believed in Him alone; placed their trust in His sacrifice alone for salvation], *to them He gave the right to become children of God* (John 1:12*a*).

So far, Mary and Joseph have carefully followed all that the Law required, and even more. They have attended ceremonies of identification and redemption.

But there was one more ceremony required by the Law.

The Ceremony of Purification

According to the Law, Mary was unclean following the birth of Jesus. After forty days, she would be required to bring two sacrifices to the priest:

1. A lamb or turtledove would atone for her defilement of having touched blood in the delivering of her child.

2. The second turtledove restored her communion with God and allowed her to participate in the temple.

The idea that Mary was above the need for personal atonement, that she was sinless and beyond the need for redemption, and that she was received into heaven after living a life of sinless perfection are simply not in the Bible. Those ideas also come from apocryphal writings.

The Bible, instead, clearly presents Mary as a sinner, calling Christ her Savior *(Luke 1:47)*. And Mary is described in *Luke 2* as following the biblical prescription for atonement and cleansing.

Mary was in need of a sacrifice for her own defilement, too; the woman who delivered the Redeemer would need to be delivered by Him.

She is bringing sacrifices—not for Jesus, not for Joseph, but for *herself*.

In other words, bearing the perfect, sinless Son of God and bringing Him into the world did not make her sinless; it actually defiled her like any other woman of a newborn. Mary was not exempt from the Law. If she and her husband didn't have the money for a lamb, she would be allowed to bring two pigeons or turtledoves. They were the only birds allowed by the Law as sacrificial gifts.[7]

The fact that Joseph and Mary brought birds instead of a lamb further indicates their financial condition.

She would have been ushered to the gate nearest the sanctuary, just beyond the Court of Women, where she would have presented her two birds to the priest for an offering. She would have stood there watching in the distance as the smoke of her offering ascended to God as she held in her arms the *final* Sacrifice.

She couldn't afford to buy a lamb to give to the priest for her atonement; but she held in her arms the *final* sacrificial Lamb, born for the final day of full and perfect atonement.

After presenting the two birds as offerings, Mary and Joseph were finished. They might have slipped away unnoticed had God not designated two witnesses to be on hand to testify that the Messiah had come.

Prophetical Confirmation

One of these witnesses was Simeon, ***righteous and devout, looking for the consolation*** [the advocate] ***of Israel*** (Luke 2:25).

Some scholars believe Simeon was the son of the famous rabbi Hillel and the father of Gamaliel, the Apostle Paul's tutor. This was the same Simeon who became a leading member of the Sanhedrin in AD 13. It's intriguing that the Mishna (the commentary on Jewish life and procedure) would one day relate many accounts of their greatest rabbis but completely ignore one of their most famous: Simeon. Why? Most likely because his faith in Jesus Christ would have been an embarrassment to them.[8]

Simeon's name literally means *hearing*, and he was evidently listening. In fact, **Luke 2:26** tells us that the Spirit of God had promised Simeon that he would not die until he had seen Israel's Messiah.

So you can imagine how, for years, Simeon would come to the temple, looking at all the babies and quietly asking himself, *Is this the One? Maybe that's the Child? Those folks look like they're carrying a newborn; I wonder if he's the One?*[9]

There's no telling how many young couples he'd met and, turning away, was inwardly disappointed.

But not this time.

When Simeon met Joseph and Mary, the Spirit of God prompted him that their newborn was indeed the Messiah. Luke gives us the touching event as Simeon ***took Him*** [Jesus] ***into his arms, and blessed God*** (Luke 2:28*b*).

This baby was the One.

Anna, the second witness and a prophetess, comes up to add her words and affirm the authenticity of Jesus the Messiah. In fact, she carries her testimony all around the temple grounds, telling everyone the good news of Christ's coming.

What incredible joy . . . and what a commotion, too. This was quite a disturbance compared to the usual buzz of activity on the temple grounds.

There stands Simeon, holding the Newborn. And he says,

> ***"Now Lord, you are releasing Your bondservant to depart in peace, according to Your word;*** [in other words, I'm ready to die now. Why?] ***for my eyes have seen Your salvation which You have prepared in the presence of all peoples, a light of revelation to the Gentiles, and the glory of your people Israel"*** (Luke 2:29–32).

The Presentation of the Lamb

"I've seen the Savior and now I'm prepared to die"—literally translated: "I've seen salvation with *my own eyes* and now I can die in peace."

There's truth in that for all of us, by the way. No one is ready to die until, by faith, they've seen the Savior—until they have embraced His truth with arms of faith.

No one is ready to encounter the valley of the shadow of death unless they have first seen the light of revelation in the person of this Child who had come as the Light of the world **(John 8:12)**.

Are you prepared to die?

You really aren't until you have believed in this One—Jehovah, Salvation, Deliverer, Yeshua—Jesus, the Messiah.

As the priests went about their duties and the people brought in their sacrifices, in the midst of it all was God incarnate—God the Son. He had taken on flesh so that He could die as the final sacrifice for sin and redeem His people: those who will place their faith in Him alone . . . forever.

Can you see them there in the courtyard? Joseph, Mary, Anna—curious people gathering around to take a peek, perhaps a priest or two—and Simeon, holding the Baby in his arms while tears of joy run down his cheeks.

> *Hope has hands.*
> *Freedom has feet.*
> *Truth will stand.*
> *The Word will speak.*

Beyond Bethlehem

The Holy and lowly will finally embrace,
For love has a heartbeat,
And grace has a face.

Compassion has a tear.
Joy has a laughter.
And here ever after, peace has a smile.
Redemption's blood has veins to flow in,
A temple to glow in.
Light is a Child.[10]

ISRAEL'S MOST WANTED

Matthew 2

At the height of World War II, as Adolph Hitler's bombers pummeled England, Winston Churchill could be heard on the radio, broadcasting his stubborn refusal to surrender. He continually encouraged the British people to fight on.

Recently, I had an opportunity to go down into the underground bunker under the streets of London where Churchill and his cabinet directed the war effort. I toured that underground war center, complete with bunk rooms and kitchen and saw the closet-sized room and the very telephone from which Winston Churchill spoke with President Roosevelt. Everyone's desk had been left exactly as it was at the end of the war.

Most importantly, I was able to view the room from which Churchill delivered those wartime messages, famously declaring, "We shall go on to the end. We shall fight in the seas and oceans, we shall fight with growing confidence in the air; we shall defend our island, whatever the cost may be; we shall never surrender . . . and I have nothing to offer you but blood, toil, tears, and sweat."[1]

Can you imagine promoting Christianity with that kind of vocabulary? Christ offers you nothing but blood, toil, tears, and sweat.

I wonder how many would sign up and join in. Maybe it's time to witness to people and tell them that if they follow Christ, He will demand they carry a cross.

With our culture's growing animosity toward the Church, Christians are becoming frightened and even angered that their convictions and freedoms are no longer being respected.

Have we forgotten that we're in a spiritual war? When did God ever say the world would be our friend? When did the Church ever receive a promise from Christ that the world would respect our convictions?

Frankly, we have lived in the lap of luxury and freedom and, unfortunately, the Church has come to believe these are her *rights*.

Turn on the television and watch pseudo pastors and false teachers peddle their promises and promote their self-serving lies that the narrow path is an easy one.

No wonder people today, especially in America, who decide to follow Jesus are surprised when they're effectively handed a shield and a helmet.

Jesus Christ actually promised, ***"I will build my church and the gates of hell shall not prevail against it"*** (Matthew 16:18 KJV). This implies that hell will certainly try!

Perhaps it's time to publicize Christianity by rediscovering the life of Christ as it really was, even in His earliest days. We're told that Christ learned obedience through the things He suffered *(Hebrews 5:8)*.

So if Christ, the perfect Man, the sinless Savior, experienced difficulties and challenges and temptation and testing, and He felt all the depths of abandonment and misunderstanding and accusation, along with financial needs and hunger and sleepless nights and weariness of mind, body, and soul . . . who are we to demand anything less—or something else?

The shadow of the cross did not fall across the path of Christ when He turned thirty years of age. No, the shadow of the conflict between heaven and hell—bringing blood and toil and tears and sweat—came much earlier than that.

At eight days of age, He cried out in pain as He was inducted into the family of Abraham's covenant keepers through circumcision. At just over a month old, He was presented at the temple and redeemed according to the Law with five hard-earned shekels that Joseph could barely afford to give.

Then, before they had settled into the normal lifestyle of the other villagers, visitors arrived with an announcement that will cause this family to eventually go into hiding.

The opening lines of *Matthew 2* declare that the Magi have arrived in Jerusalem. These men were the spiritual descendants of a revered wise man named Daniel, who centuries earlier had left a legacy of faith and a litany of facts for those who longed for the coming Messiah. The Magi had arrived after their long journey out of Babylon—the land of ancient Persia.

They appeared with an earth-shaking question that should have stopped everyone in their tracks:

> ***Where is He who has been born King of the Jews? For we saw His star in the east and have come to worship Him"*** (Matthew 2:2).

Shekinah Glory in the Heavens

There are some who believe this *star* was a conjunction of Jupiter and Saturn. Others believe that an arrangement of stars made the sign of the fish. Some say this star was a low-hanging meteor or an erratic comet.

I believe it was nothing less than the Shekinah glory. Both the Hebrew *kokab* and the Greek *aster* are words for star, and both are used to represent any great brilliance or radiance.[2]

His star was nothing more than a bright supernatural light—nothing less than the radiant Shekinah glory of God's presence, which explains how it seems to turn on and off at certain times:

- the glory of God's radiant light already observed by the shepherds as the angels sang *(Luke 2:9)*;
- the divine pillar of fire by night *(Exodus 13:21)*;
- the consuming fire on the mountaintop *(Exodus 24:17)*;
- the shining face of Christ, like the sun, on the Mount of Transfiguration *(Matthew 17:2)*;
- the brilliant light that blinded Saul on the Damascus road *(Acts 9:3)*;
- the promised star that would come forth from Jacob *(Numbers 24:17)*;
- the Bright and Morning Star (Christ) at the end of the New Testament in the Book of Revelation *(Revelation 22:16)*.

The Shekinah glory hovers above Jerusalem; the Magi arrive—then the light turns off. That forces the wise men to go to the king and ask their startling question.

Why didn't God just lead them with His Shekinah glory to the home of Joseph and Mary to begin with? Because there were prophecies to fulfill in this incarnation; furthermore, this drama is destined to include blood, toil, tears, and sweat.

In *Matthew 2:5*, the chief priests and scribes tell Herod that the Messiah is to be born in Bethlehem . . . so, to Bethlehem the wise men are directed.

By the way, an astral conjunction, a meteor, or a comet would not be able to identify a specific house:

> ***After coming into the house they saw the Child with Mary His mother*** (Matthew 2:11).

Not only is the family of Jesus living in a house when the Magi arrive, Jesus isn't a baby anymore. In fact, Matthew writes of the Child (*paidion*—a Greek word that can refer to a newborn but, most often, signifies a little child).[3]

The Bible states that the wise men did not come into a stable; it was a house. This is not a manger scene with a baby—this is a living room scene with a toddler.

If you track the boyhood of Jesus carefully, you discover that Luke's Gospel has included the details of His birth in a Bethlehem stable—more than likely, a cave or, perhaps, an outer courtyard for animals. Luke also records Jesus' presentation at the temple a month later.

Now, Matthew fills in the narrative: Joseph and Mary have decided to stay in Bethlehem. And why not?— they've left behind a scandal. They have a quick and unorthodox marriage; Mary's premarital pregnancy and their departure together to Bethlehem meant one thing: the scandal they had created and the shame brought on their families was best left alone.

They would never go back.

Joseph either found a home to rent or—this is more probable—he built a simple hut on borrowed land, according to the customs of their culture.

Jesus is now a toddler. And while Joseph is away on some construction project, the Magi show up unexpectedly.

Wise Men in Bethlehem

The arrival of the wise men and their entourage outside this simple home was made possible by that Shekinah glory which **stood over the place where the Child was** (Matthew 2:9*b*).

Once inside, Matthew tells us that as soon as the Magi saw Jesus, **they fell to the ground and worshiped Him** (Matthew 2:11*b*).

And they gave Him gifts—each steeped in symbolic truth:

1. **gold** – Seneca, the Roman philosopher and writer who lived during the days of Christ, said that in Persia no one would approach a king without a gift, and gold was the proper gift for the King of men.[4]
2. **frankincense** – a substance used in temple worship to serve as fragrant offerings between man and God. This gift wonderfully illustrated the role of High Priest that Christ would have to this very day, interceding between God and man.

3. **myrrh** – a substance used for embalming the dead. No doubt, this gift was a gift of faith to the One who had come to suffer and die.[5]

The shadow of the cross fell over that little living room as these kingmakers gave the God-toddler the gifts that declared He was King, High Priest, and Suffering Savior.

Maniac in Jerusalem

Now the wise men had promised Herod that they would return and give him the street address so he could go and worship the Messiah, too, just as he had requested. But the Magi were warned by God in a dream not to return to Herod *(Matthew 2:12)*.

A closer look at Herod will easily explain why.

Herod had been awarded by the Roman senate the title "King of the Jews." He wasn't the kind of dictator who shared his toys or his titles.

Herod began his reign in 40 BC. He had done a lot of good things for the Jewish people as he attempted to win their devotion. He rebuilt the temple, returned taxes to the people during difficult times, built theatres and race tracks for entertainment, and developed seaports for better commerce.

By the time Jesus was born, Herod was an old man and, historians tell us, afflicted with venereal diseases and, for the most part, insane. In fact, in his later years, Herod had become insanely jealous of his throne; he murdered every rival.

A descendant of Esau (an Edomite), he married Mariamne, a Jewess from an aristocratic family which, he again hoped, would win him popularity among the Jews.

In his growing paranoia, however, he later murdered her 17-year-old brother and then had her executed. He even put to death several of his own sons in order to stamp out any threat of assassination.

Herod was a sadistic killer who slaughtered officials, generals, senators, soldiers, and citizens whom he suspected of any disloyalty.

On one occasion a faithful soldier confided to Herod that many within the ranks hated his cruelty and sided with his sons; officers openly cursed him. While this soldier thought the information would gain him favor with Herod, the emperor, instead, ordered the man put on the rack and stretched until he cried out name after name of the traitors. He even confessed the names of innocent men—anything to stop the torture—but Herod pressed the guards to continue until the man died. Then all the accused were rounded up and torn to pieces while Herod, livid with rage, jumped up and down as he screamed for them to die.[6]

No wonder the Roman emperor Caesar Augustus, who had made Herod king over this region of the empire, remarked on one occasion that he would rather be Herod's swine than Herod's son.[7]

Can you now imagine the wise men arriving in Jerusalem and asking the question, "Where is the young

King of the Jews living?" They had no idea the firestorm they would ignite by their simple question; they didn't know the man they had come before was a madman.

But don't miss the irony here: the only man in this scene who actually believed the wise men had a legitimate purpose in coming to Jerusalem was Herod! He was the only one who took them seriously.

Every rabbi and priest should have rushed to join the Magi on their journey to Bethlehem. Instead, you discover in this paragraph of Scripture the three most common responses to the Gospel of Jesus Christ, the message that He was born, lived a sinless life, died on the cross to pay the penalty for sin, and then rose from the dead and is coming back to reign on planet Earth:

1. **Hostility and pride** – "There is no king but me; I will abdicate my throne for no one; I will surrender my will to none other than me, myself, and I."

2. **Indifference and religious activity, as usual** – "The Messiah is going to be born in Bethlehem? That's fine, now move along—we've got sacrifices to prepare and traditions to protect. You're in my way here . . . and I certainly don't have time to traipse off to Bethlehem."

3. **Worship and personal sacrifice** – Imagine the scene as the Magi came to the house: Joseph is evidently out working; Mary's there with her little

Toddler; the Magi walk inside and kneel before Him in worship.

They give Him gifts, and because He's just a normal toddler, He probably isn't interested in the gifts—He's more interested in the boxes. Then again, perhaps He never came out from hiding behind His mother's robe.

What happens next in this chapter is the fulfillment of three prophecies. They are among the few clues and insights that we have into the boyhood of Jesus.

Flight into Egypt

Now when they [the Magi] ***had gone, behold, an angel of the Lord appeared to Joseph in a dream and said, "Get up! Take the Child and His mother and flee to Egypt, and remain there until I tell you; for Herod is going to search for the Child to destroy Him"*** (Matthew 2:13).

Once Herod realized the Magi had tricked him and traveled back home on a different interstate, he could only assume that they had warned the parents of Jesus, as well.[8]

The angelic warning came in the middle of the night. "Joseph, get up," which meant Joseph didn't finish his rest—neither did Mary or Jesus. "Get up, now! Get your family ready . . . have Mary to hurry and get Jesus dressed . . . *run!*"

The aorist tenses of these verbs indicate single acts. In the middle of the night: get up, get Mary and Jesus, and run for your lives.

Joseph didn't have time to pack a cart with the furniture he'd recently finished; Mary would have to leave the crib and grab only what she could wear or carry and race out the door.

The warning was terrifying and real . . . Herod was coming!

But where were they to go? The angel had fortunately divulged their escape route and destination: Egypt. Wait, that's another country! God knew that and kindly implied through His angelic messenger that they would stay there ***until I tell you.***

> ***So Joseph got up and took the Child and His mother while it was still night, and left for Egypt. He remained there until the death of Herod. This was to fulfill what had been spoken by the Lord through the prophet: "Out of Egypt I called My Son"*** (Matthew 2:14).

This was no flower-strewn pathway for them . . . this was another call to blood, toil, tears, and sweat.

Have you ever taken your family on a trip? How much did you prepare? How much did you pack? Was it just one suitcase per person (good luck!)?

On several occasions my wife and I have traveled to foreign countries . . . like Minnesota. Well, all right, to places like France, Austria, England, and Switzerland. Talk about a packing process . . . and traveling dates . . . and schedules.

Money? Yep!

Passports? In my pocket!

Tickets? Got 'em!

Itinerary? In my briefcase!

Carry-ons? All ready!

Something to read on the journey? Absolutely.

And I even remembered a pack of gum for that ear-popping descent of the Boeing 777.

When we've traveled, we've been able to choose the most convenient time to depart; we already know where we'll be staying when we get there; it's all mapped out ahead of time.

Just imagine the middle of the night there in a Bethlehem hut: get up . . . get dressed . . . run.

Surely the foreknowledge of God would have allowed Joseph and Mary plenty of time to pack.

Surely this isn't the way God would map it out for His chosen One!

But it was.

Slip into the middle of God's will for Joseph and Mary. No time for planning; no map; no choice of departure times; no time to pack just the right things.

In fact, in **Matthew 2:13**, the word for *flee* in the English Bible is from the Greek word *pheugo*, which means "to seek safety in flight." It's the same Greek word that gives us our transliterated English word fugitive.[9]

In other words, "Joseph and Mary, run for your lives! You have just become Israel's most wanted fugitives!"

Why? Because Herod wants to kill your little Boy.

The grammar in this text indicates that their flight is the beginning of action that is to be continued. They were not to stop until they were safely within Egypt's borders and beyond the reach of Herod. From Bethlehem to the border of Egypt was 75 miles.[10]

Joseph was given no specific address—he wasn't told the directions for the safest route there, where they would be staying, or if anyone would be waiting for them when they arrived—just to run!

Now? *Now!* In the middle of the night!

But wait . . . God could have protected Joseph and his little family right under the vain nose of Herod. He could have deposed Herod and killed the soldiers; He could have blinded those soldiers. God could have miraculously hidden the family like a suitcase of smuggled Bibles that the communist guards never see. He could have . . . but He didn't.

God chose to protect them by the very ordinary and unremarkable means of *flight*. The will of God meant hardship and suffering, but He would sustain them through it.

The message for them to run was supernatural—the word from God had arrived in a dream. This parallel occurs to me: the Word of God has arrived to us in a Book—supernaturally inspired.

Still, as we take steps in obedience, all our questions aren't answered, and neither were theirs. God did *not* do something for Joseph and Mary that He withholds from us.

Once again, the Medieval church just couldn't imagine this being the will of God for Joseph and Mary. So the apocryphal writings compiled legends and myths to make it look a lot less like they had to endure suffering and hardship for their obedience.

One legend recorded this story about Joseph, Mary, and Jesus needing a place to sleep one night as they traveled toward Egypt. They sought refuge in a cave where it so cold that the ground was covered with frost. Fortunately, a little spider recognized Jesus and wished so much that he could do something to keep Him warm that he spun his web across the entrance of the cave so thick that it hung like a curtain, and the cave became warm and cozy.[11]

Other ancient traditions imagined that when they arrived at a grove of fruit trees, Jesus commanded the trees to bend down so Joseph could pluck the fruit with ease. Jesus then ordered a spring of water to gush from the roots of the tree to quench their thirst. Mary was even able to sleep because an angel arrived to play hymns on the violin.

Wherever they traveled, animals would bow and pay homage to them and idols would crumble to dust whenever they passed.

Their journey to Egypt was more like a triumphal entry... a holiday trip with fruit, water, nice animals, and violin music to soothe their weary bodies and minds.

That's the kind of travel experience we would desire for Jesus and His parents, but . . .

Their stay in Egypt was riddled with supposed myths and legends that reveal how wonderful their time was while away. Take, for instance, the legend of Mary washing the swaddling clothes of Baby Jesus in their Egyptian home. By the way, Jesus was too old at the time for swaddling clothes (diapers), but don't let that get in the way of a good legend! As she hung the linen out to dry, a demon-possessed boy came by and brushed up against them and was instantly freed from the demon.

In my study I came across several more traditions that included special power from Jesus' bath water. Evidently it was strong enough to heal a princess of leprosy . . . and anybody else who came in contact with it.

According to these legends and the apocryphal writings, Egypt was a vacation for the fugitives. Every need was instantly met and suffering and hardship were eliminated, not only in their lives but in everyone's life around them. Little Jesus just kept performing miracle after miracle.

We are clearly told in ***John 2:11*** that the turning of water into wine at the wedding feast in Cana was the *first* miracle Jesus performed—*the first attesting sign of His deity* (the *arche* *semeion*)—the *beginning* of His miracles which He first displayed in Cana as He began His ministry at the age of thirty.[12]

The truth is there were no special miracles to turn Egypt into a minor paradise. There was no special bath water, no fruit trees, no water to drink on command. God never promised Joseph and Mary these kinds of benefits for their simple obedience.

God hasn't promised to turn our Egypt into paradise, either.

The escape of Joseph and Mary and their God-toddler from Bethlehem that night on their long flight to Egypt was the same kind of journey that any ordinary family would have had to endure. In fact, it was all the more difficult because they were now Israel's "Most Wanted."

We can only imagine the fear during their several days of traveling: Joseph looking over his shoulder every other minute; hearing clattering hooves behind every hilltop; wanting to stop and rest longer than can be allowed; their hearts never really stop pounding all the way to Egypt . . . and they have to be asking, "Why?"

God's angel actually told them why; this would be the fulfillment of one of many prophecies that validated the authenticity of the claim of Messiah. God said that Jesus would ***come out of Egypt*** . . . and now Egypt becomes their hiding place until Herod dies.

Jesus would become the illustration of Israel's calling from that same country. Israel was often spoken of in the

Old Testament as the son of God *(Hosea 11:1)*. So *the* Son of God illustrates Israel's deliverance. But there's even more to it than that: Christ embodies the Deliverer from Egypt.

There had been another deliverer born in Egypt. By his parents' quick action, he also had avoided a death warrant from a king. That king—Pharaoh—had even ordered the killing of all the Jewish male babies, and Moses was hidden away by his parents. He survived and eventually led his people out of bondage.

Jesus the Deliverer is referred to as the *greater* Moses in *Hebrews 3*. They both came out of Egypt, and they both led their people out of bondage; but the deliverance of Moses was temporary and insufficient—the deliverance of Jesus Christ is eternal and all-sufficient.

Bloodbath in Bethlehem

Yet another prophecy will be fulfilled as this family flees to Egypt:

> *Then when Herod saw that he had been tricked by the magi, he became very enraged, and sent and slew all the male children who were in Bethlehem and all its vicinity, from two years old and under, according to the time which he had determined from the magi. Then what had been spoken through Jeremiah the prophet was fulfilled: "A voice*

was heard in Ramah, weeping and great mourning, Rachel weeping for her children; and she refused to be comforted, because they were no more" (Matthew 2:16–18).

The actions of Herod literally defy imagination. He's around 70 years of age, diseased, crippled, infected with untreatable venereal diseases. Historical sources reveal that his intestines are literally rotting away; his bodyguards have to rotate frequently because they cannot bear the stench emanating from the pores of his skin. His physicians can't heal him; the warm baths cannot soothe him; his body is covered with ulcers and his legs are too swollen for him to walk.

But no king will have *his* throne! Even though he knows his death is imminent, he clutches his crown. He is the perfect picture of depraved, stubborn mankind.

One of his final orders was to round up hundreds of prominent Jewish citizens. They were arrested and incarcerated inside the arena on trumped-up charges. He then gave the order that on the day he died, these Jews were to be killed. The statement he is said to have uttered has transcended the centuries: "When I die, the Jews may not mourn me but, by the gods, they *will* mourn."[13]

And for now, there is great weeping in Bethlehem. Historical demographers estimate that there were at least thirty or more children under the age of two in Bethlehem and the surrounding area.

Instead of the religious leaders and rabbis and scribes rushing to Bethlehem to crown the young Messiah as their king, the soldiers of Herod stampede into town and rip little boys from their mothers' arms and put them to death.

Rachel is weeping for her children. This prophecy harkened to the time when all Jewish mothers wept over Israel's great tragedy in the days of Jeremiah. This text also tells us that their weeping was an Old Testament foreshadowing of the mothers in Bethlehem who would weep bitterly over the massacre of their little boys at the hands of Herod's men.[14]

But what makes Herod's crime even more wicked is the fact that he knew that the little boy he was trying to kill was the Messiah.

Herod is nothing less than a first-century antichrist—a pawn in the hands of Satan attempting to destroy the seed of the woman: the virgin-born Messiah.

And as the mothers wept in Bethlehem, Herod died in Jerusalem.

By the way, his sister and her husband who were supposed to signal the soldiers to murder the Jews in the arena went, instead, and opened the doors and set those Jewish captives free.

Another ironic illustration? I don't think so, for when the *final* antichrist is killed, the Jewish nation will also be set free.

There was the escape into Egypt *(Matthew 2:15)* and the bloodbath in Bethlehem *(Matthew 2:18)*, and now there is one more prophecy to be fulfilled in these days of Christ's childhood.

Nobodies in Nazareth

It isn't my desire to be disrespectful, but Joseph, Mary, and Jesus were nobodies living nowhere. That's exactly what they were considered . . . and that's exactly where we find them living after another visit from an angel:

> *But when Herod died, behold, an angel of the Lord appeared in a dream to Joseph in Egypt, and said, "Get up, take the Child and His mother, and go into the land of Israel"* (Matthew 2:19-20).

In the middle of the night. Sound familiar? Here we go again. Poor Joseph will never lie down without wondering, *Am I gonna make it through the night.*

The difference in this verse is the lack of urgency. There's no need to run, hurry, or hide. In fact, Matthew says that Joseph was clearly reassured of that:

> *"[T]hose who sought the Child's life are dead." So Joseph got up, took the Child and His mother, and came into the land of Israel* (Matthew 2:20*b*–21).

Their weeks and months of hiding in Egypt are over. Jesus is still called a *paidion* (child), so we know He's still a little boy when Joseph is told to return to Israel.

But then Matthew adds:

> ***But when he** [Joseph] **heard that Archelaus was reigning over Judea in place of his father Herod, he was afraid to go there*** (Matthew 2:22).

The text implies that *while they are on their way*, Joseph learned that Herod's son Archelaus has been given the throne. Archelaus was in many ways worse than his father. In fact, he inaugurated his reign by killing 3,000 Jews in the temple during Passover. His reign was so cruel that even Augustus, the Roman emperor—no saint himself—finally banished him after nine years of atrocities.

Joseph had every reason to be afraid. So God came to him again in a dream and told him specifically to settle in the regions of Galilee, and Joseph moved his family and settled down in Nazareth. And guess what?

> ***This was to fulfill what was spoken through the prophets: "He shall be called a Nazarene"*** (Matthew 2:23).

Nazareth was located about 55 miles north of Jerusalem. The inhabitants in these Galilean regions were people known for being rough, uneducated, and even uncivilized.

This was an insignificant village . . . just a common place filled with common, ordinary people trying to make a living.

The earthly origins of Christ were as challenging and difficult as you can imagine: an outdoor shelter for a birthplace; his parents on the run as fugitives, immigrating to Egypt and then back to Israel where they lived their lives in obscurity.

But what character. Joseph and Mary exemplified incredible obedience and perseverance—all this in the midst of confusion and fear and danger. I can't imagine the desperation they felt as they clung to the brief announcements from heaven. There weren't many details provided in this journey of faith as they moved from place . . . to place . . . to place.

Jesus Christ is one of us, and yet, His boyhood was far more commonplace than any of ours.

Three thoughts struck me as I worked through this unfolding drama:

1. The **will of God** does not circumvent the challenges of life.
2. The **leading of God** does not eliminate attacks by the enemy.
3. The **promises of God** do not lessen the responsibilities of the believer.

How easy to think that the will of God and the leading of God and the promises of God result in **closeness to God**, and closeness to God would *never* translate into blood, toil, tears, and sweat.

Surely, the *godly* life is a good life, and all goes smoothly.

Well, here you have it, spelled out in the early days of Baby/Toddler Jesus, His God-ordained mother, and His God-appointed stepfather, who were:

- instructed by an angel;
- assured of God's promises;
- enveloped by God's love;
- fully obedient to God's will;
- living out the prophecies of old.

Their lives were a fulfillment of God's promises to the world! And what did they encounter?

Blood, toil, tears, and sweat.

My hat goes off to them. In fact, I have come to greatly appreciate this young couple through this brief exposition. What surrender . . . what perseverance to keep getting up and moving forward at God's command.

Time and time again, they changed everything about their lives to accommodate the word from God . . . and to fulfill the prophecies of God.

One author wrote that while traveling in England, he saw the tombstone of an old Cavalier soldier who had lost his property and then his life in a battle defending King Charles. The epitaph read: He served King Charles with a constant, dangerous, and expensive loyalty.[15]

What a great testimony for the Christian who allows the shadow of the cross to fall across their pathway. This is the testimony of true allegiance: to serve our King with a constant, dangerous, and expensive loyalty, no matter what . . . even if it includes a call to blood, toil, tears, and sweat.

MISSING!

Luke 2:41-51

Most Jewish calendars had several dates circled in red—dates no faithful Jew ever wanted to miss. One of the most anticipated arrived in springtime and was, without a doubt, the most exciting annual festival of all: the Feast of Unleavened Bread, or Passover.

Jewish law actually required all men from age thirteen and up to attend three feasts in Jerusalem: Passover, Pentecost, and Tabernacles.[1] During this Passover feast, we're given another fascinating glimpse into the boyhood of Jesus.

Luke begins the narrative by telling us that Jesus and ***His parents went to Jerusalem every year at the Feast of the Passover*** (Luke 2:41). This verse allows us to view the family home of Jesus, and what we see is remarkable devotion to God.

The Law allowed any Jewish male who lived beyond 15 miles of Jerusalem to celebrate Passover in his own village and not have to make a lengthy and expensive journey.[2] Nazareth is about 65 miles north of Jerusalem, so Joseph is well outside the 15-mile perimeter. In fact, it would have taken several days of travel and time away from his business and responsibilities. It would be costly.

We should also know that the Law did *not* require women to attend any of the feasts in Jerusalem, and in this culture they most often stayed behind to care for the children and tend the livestock and garden.

Still, it would have been the desire for every godly Jewish man *and* woman to travel to Jerusalem—the heart of their nation—and enter into these celebrations of national life and faith.

We know from history that every faithful Jew wanted to celebrate the Feasts in Jerusalem at least once during their lifetime . . . most would be satisfied with that.

With all these facts in mind, notice key clues about the passion and devotion of Joseph and Mary:

- ***Now His* parents** – both Joseph *and* Mary
- ***went to* Jerusalem** – they embraced the costly trip in order to celebrate in the capital city
- **every year *at the feast of Passover*** – not just once in their lifetime but *every* year!

What insight into their personal sacrifice and dedication to the worship of the living God.

And this particular year will be especially significant, according to Luke's account, because Jesus is twelve years old. He's only months away from full membership into the synagogue as a 13-year-old.

According to the Mishnah (a commentary of every aspect of Jewish living during the days of Christ), fathers were encouraged to include their sons in the observance of the Passover "one or two years before they were of age." This was the age of thirteen, when they became officially "sons of the Law"—that is, personally old enough to be considered responsible to keep God's law for themselves.[3]

So here is 12-year-old Jesus, overflowing with energy and curiosity, accompanying Joseph and Mary as they fulfill their annual pilgrimage to Jerusalem to celebrate with their people the atoning work of God through the Passover lamb.

What irony . . . they are bringing the Deliverer to Jerusalem as the people celebrate their deliverance from Egypt. Mary and Joseph are bringing the final Passover Lamb to celebrate the Feast of the Passover lambs.

In the City

Jerusalem was packed with pilgrims; merchants lined the streets with their booths to sell their wares. But the most intense activity was at the sheep stalls where the Jewish pilgrims bartered for sheep to sacrifice at the temple.[4]

Joseph, Mary and the Boy Jesus went to the stalls to choose their lamb. Can you imagine Joseph asking Jesus to pick one out—the Lamb choosing a lamb for sacrifice.

Keep in mind that there were shepherds still living who had been keeping the temple sheep (the paschal lambs) in Bethlehem that night when the angels had appeared with the good news of Christ's birth. The sheep in those flocks would be driven later to Jerusalem for the Passover.

The same year Jesus and His parents picked out their lamb for the Feast, one historical record indicates that more than 250,000 sheep had been driven into the city for that very purpose!

There were a million or more Jewish pilgrims crammed into the city as the sun rose on Passover Day. All 24 divisions (instead of just one) of priests were serving in the temple. And they would be busy every single moment during this festival season.

Jesus would watch as his stepfather killed the lamb and a priest caught the blood in a silver or golden basin and then threw the blood at the foot of the altar. Joseph would have prepared the lamb as the Levite choirs sang ***Psalms 113–118***.

Then Joseph would have carried the lamb over his shoulder and walked with Jesus and Mary to wherever they were staying that night. They would prepare the lamb for supper. Jesus would have asked his stepfather the ceremonial question that night, "Why is this night different from all other nights?" And Joseph would have answered with the story of the deliverance of the Jewish people from Egypt, led by Moses their deliverer.

The night would end late and many people would take to the streets in joyful celebration and have reunions with friends and family. Others would wait for the opening of the doors on the Temple Mount at midnight, where they could go for further worship and prayer.[5]

The celebration lasted for an entire week. Most Jews came for the significant two-day portion of the ceremony, which included the Passover meal.[6]

But not this family!

Luke records that *they were returning, after spending the full number of days* (Luke 2:43a). In other words, they stayed the entire week—they weren't about to miss one moment.

In a Panic

Evidently, Jesus couldn't get enough either. Luke writes:

> [T]*he boy Jesus stayed behind in Jerusalem. But His parents were unaware of it but supposed Him to be in the* **minivan** (Luke 2: 43b–44a).

Well, "minivan" isn't exactly what it says, but it's the same idea as the ***caravan***.

It was the custom for women and children to travel in the front of the caravan and the men to travel behind it, making sure no one got lost along the way. The two sections would meet up in the evening when they made camp.

Joseph thought Jesus was with Mary, and Mary obviously thought Jesus was with Joseph. As they gathered in camp that evening, only then did they realize that Jesus wasn't with either one of them—and He wasn't with any of the other families, either.

It finally hit them: "We left Jesus in Jerusalem!"

Have you ever left your child somewhere? Did you ever get home from church and realize you were one kid short?

But this wasn't just *any* kid . . .

"Honey, do you know where the Savior of the world is?"

"No, I thought He was with you!"

"Me? I thought *you* had Him!"

"Oh, no, we've lost the Messiah!"

CBS Online ran a story about a mother forgetting to take her son home after a birthday party at Chuck E. Cheese. I can understand the oversight . . . you can lose an elephant inside that place.

But what made this all the more interesting was that it was *his* birthday party. The party went just fine. The problem came when all the children and adults climbed into three different vehicles and headed home. Everyone got in but Michael, the birthday boy. Apparently the six-year-old returned to the play area and was left behind. Employees found Michael wandering around the restaurant when they closed at ten o'clock. Michael's mother had assumed that her son was staying with his grandmother and didn't even know he was missing until the next morning.[7]

Now it's one thing to lose your child and not know he's missing until he shows up again. It's another thing to lose your child and know it . . . but not know exactly where he is.

That was Mary and Joseph.

In the Temple

That realization grows into a three-day, panic-stricken search:

> ***When they did not find Him, they returned to Jerusalem looking for Him. Then, after three days they found Him in the temple*** (Luke 2:45–46*a*).

Now, there are some who think this reflects poorly on Joseph and Mary as parents. I don't think so. It may be nothing more than the fact that they had perfect confidence in Jesus that they didn't ask Him who He was planning to travel with back to Nazareth . . . they were sure He would be where He was supposed to be.[8]

Others believe this reflects poorly on Jesus. In fact, some have concluded that Jesus sinned; He had disobediently run away to "join the circus," so to speak.

That's out of the question. A sinful Jesus would contradict the clear record of Scripture:

- He was tempted in every way, just as we are, yet without sin ***(Hebrews 4:15)***;
- He was holy, blameless, pure, and set apart from sinners ***(Hebrews 7:26)***;
- The Lord committed no sin ***(1 Peter 2:22)***;
- And in Him is no sin ***(1 John 3:5)***.

That doesn't mean that Jesus was incapable of *unknowingly* going against His parent's wishes—like any other middle schooler who is not mature enough to understand. However, as a sinless being, He was incapable of *knowingly* rebelling.

At this point in the boyhood of Jesus, He was both fully God the Son and fully a 12-year-old boy.

The Holy Spirit, in concert with Christ's divine nature, was protecting Him from sinning in even the slightest manner. Still, as a normal 12-year-old boy, He was able to fully embrace the human experience and emotion and learning curve, which even included making mistakes.

Jesus stubbed his toe; He left the door open; He didn't think through consequences, just as normal 12-year-olds sometimes fail to do.

Was He fully human? Absolutely! Was He then ever silly? Did He ever do something dumb or dangerous? Did He make mistakes? Was He immature at times? Was He ever unaware of consequences or naïve in His actions?

Without a doubt!

This is the mystery of the incarnation: He was fully God *and* fully human—two natures coexisting within His mortal frame.

Christ had a human nature but not a sinful, fallen nature. This nature, called the Adamic nature, was transmitted seminally through the father and never touched Jesus, thanks to the virgin birth of Christ.

Christ also had a divine nature, transmitted to His embryo by means of His divine conception. He was both completely equal with God the Father as deity *(Philippians 2:6)* and completely equal to the human race He had joined *(Philippians 2:7)*.

Since Jesus had a human nature, He would have had all its accompanying emotions and feelings and intuitions . . . and even growth spurts.

Being silly or dangerous or immature or unaware or naive and, maybe even at times, guilty of doing something dumb are not the same things as being *sinful.*

Jesus was everything a 12-year-old boy was . . . *except* willfully sinful.

And something major was happening to this junior-high-aged God the Son.

In Their Midst

Frankly, we have every reason to believe that it was during this Passover celebration that Jesus was given enough spiritual insight by the indwelling Holy Spirit to provoke in Him some profound realizations.

By the time Mary and Joseph caught up with Him, He knew He wasn't just *any* 12-year-old boy with a mom and a dad and a little house back in Nazareth.

For starters, when Mary and Joseph find him, Luke records their rendezvous:

> [He was] ***sitting in the midst of the teachers, both listening to them and asking them questions. And all who heard Him were amazed at His understanding and His answers*** (Luke 2:46b–47).

One author pointed out that Passover season was a time when the Sanhedrin (Jewish leaders of renown and scholarship) would meet in public to discuss religious and theological questions.[9]

That has led many to believe Jesus was captivating the highest court of Jewish law and liturgy with His questions, answers, and insights.

Jesus wasn't faking anything here. He wasn't demonstrating some sort of divine omniscience, either. He had legitimate questions as He now hit a divinely appointed growth spurt.

He also had a quick, well-studied mind with a unique perspective, which gushes out: ***they were amazed at His understanding and His answers.*** You could render that "they admired His insight and wisdom."[10]

In other words, Jesus was wise beyond His years.

So what you have here in this scene is a sinless, intelligent, well-studied middle school Boy. But more importantly, He is now being illuminated by revelation from God His Father as to His true nature and mission. We can be sure of that because of His response to Mary, which we read a couple of verses later.

In fact, right in the middle of this Q & A session with leading scholars and rabbis surrounding young Jesus, Mary and Joseph arrive on the scene. They had looked everywhere *but* the temple.

> ***When they saw Him, they were astonished; and His mother said to Him, "Son, why have You treated us this way? Behold, "Your father and I have been anxiously looking for You"*** (Luke 2:48).

I love this . . . and don't miss the fact that Mary is just as normal a mother as any. Never mind that Jesus is surrounded by the Supreme Court of Israel; never mind that He's holding them spellbound.

Mary basically blurts out, "What in the world are You doing? We've been looking all over for You—what got into you, young Man?"

I'm not Jesus, but this sure sounds familiar!

And notice that Mary doesn't have a halo around her head and perfect composure while she addresses this audience. She didn't exclaim, "Oh, there you are, Son—in the temple, of course. So, why don't You just carry on while we sit over there until You've finished Your dialogue, and then we'll all go home."

Hardly. It was more like, "Your father and I have been so anxious and worried sick . . . why would You do something like this to us?" The word *anxious* can be translated "with anguish."[11]

Frankly, we would have said the same thing . . . or worse.

Joseph and Mary had lost their Son who knows where—back in a city with hundreds of thousands of strangers; for three days they hadn't slept or eaten a bite of food.

They imagined the worst.

In the Godhead

Jesus finally responds to His parents. Get ready for His *first recorded words*—in fact, the *only* recorded words of Jesus prior to His ministry eighteen years later:

> ***And He said to them, "Why is it that you were looking for Me? Did you not know that I had to be in My Father's house*** [literally: involved in the things of My Father]***?"*** (Luke 2:49).

My goodness . . . He knows.

He knows!

One author illustrated the growth of self-conscious understanding as glowing rays of light spilling out more and more at the dawning of a new day.[12]

These two natures were not separate within Him but intertwined in mystery to us. His human nature—His human mind and heart—grew during this Feast of the Passover to understand His divine nature.

MISSING!

It seems clear that it was during *this* Passover—in the City of His father David—God the Father revealed to Him that He was God the Son.

The sun of realization rose while He was in Jerusalem.

These first recorded words of Jesus literally blow everyone's mind with His personal *possessive* reference to God as *His* Father: **"I must be about My Father's business."**

No one spoke of God as *their* Father.

In the entire Old Testament collection of 39 books, God as Father appears only 14 times and always in reference to the nation Israel. God was referred to as Abraham's Father, but Abraham never personally referred to God as "my" Father.

Nobody talked like that.

So here, at the age of twelve, Jesus now clearly knew that God was His Father in a way in which God was not Father to anyone else.[13]

He is now conscious of His own Person, His own relationship to His Father, and knows a little more about His own mission in life.[14]

I find it intriguing in the way He so innocently and naïvely said to Mary and Joseph, "I thought you knew this? You, of all people, should have seen this coming—that I would want to be about the things of My Father."

Luke delivers the reaction of Joseph and Mary:

> **But they did not understand the statement which He had made to them** (Luke 2:50).

Why would this announcement be a bit surprising and confusing to Joseph and Mary? The implication is that their Son had never said anything like this *before*. He's now speaking a different language . . . He's referring to God in a way they didn't understand or even imagine.

Joseph and Mary are, to some degree, confused about the supernatural conception of Jesus Christ. We tend to think they grasped the idea early on. By no means . . . but let's not be too hard on them.

Consider the fact that the Holy Spirit is only so named "The Holy Spirit" three times in the entire Old Testament—twice in Isaiah and once in the Psalms—and none of the verses were descriptive or explanatory.

So here comes the angel to Joseph, saying, "Go ahead and take Mary to be your wife because the Child she is carrying is conceived of the *Holy Spirit*" ***(Matthew 1:20)***.

Gabriel went to Mary and said, "You're going to have a Baby." And Mary said, "How can this happen when I've never been with a man?" And Gabriel answered, "The *Holy Spirit* will come upon you."

They were both probably wondering, *Who in the world is that?*

And now, shocking as it was to their Jewish ears under the Old Covenant, Jesus says that He's in the temple involved in the things of *His* Father.

I commend Mary and Joseph once again. Don't miss the fact that they were obedient to God in spite of being, for the most part, confused.

How many times have we said to God, "I'll do whatever You ask me to do so long as you clear up some questions *first*. I'll gladly follow You as soon as You show me what's around the next corner."

We tend to have confidence in the will of God when it's understandable. I doubt any of us would announce gushingly, "I'm right in the middle of God's will . . . and is it ever confusing!"

Joseph and Mary obeyed in spite of their confusion. In fact, children born later to Mary and Joseph will be equally confused. None of Christ's siblings believed His claims. At one point, they come to the conclusion that Jesus has lost His grip on reality *(Mark 3:21)*. Only after the resurrection of Christ from the grave will they believe in Him.

Jesus Christ had indeed come from the Father and was on earth to do His Father's will.

Some have gone on record saying that a 12-year-old would never be able to grasp so significant a reality in life—He was simply too young to formulate such a personal identity and mission.

Not true. Anyone who thinks that needs to read a few more biographies of distinctive leaders from both inside and outside the Church.

During my study, I was introduced to the life of Allen Gardiner, the founder of what became the South American Missionary Society—an organization used by God in the 1800s especially to reach South America with the Gospel.

One night in December, a little more than 200 years ago, Mrs. Gardiner entered her little boy's bedroom and found him sleeping on the cold hard floor. She woke him and put him in his bed. He protested and informed his mother that one day he was going to be traveling the world and he needed to prepare for such hardship. He was six years old.

Allen, indeed, spent his life traveling throughout South America, distributing Bibles and Christian literature. He was not well received wherever he went, often narrowly escaping with his life. Throughout Chile, Argentina, and Bolivia, he continued his mission. On one occasion he trekked 1,000 miles overland by pack mule from Buenos Aires to Santiago, distributing the Word of God. He had few converts and even fewer church plants. In his late fifties, he and his missionary teammates died while attempting to reach a new field of hostile Indians. He was found next to his boat with his journal still in his hand, in which he had written his last words, "Let not this mission fail. I beg Thee to raise up others and to send forth laborers into this harvest. Let it be seen, for the manifestation of Thy Glory and Grace that nothing is too hard for Thee.[15]

And it all began to burn in his heart at the age of six.

Jesus Christ was twelve. And He spoke with determined intentionality: "I *have* to be involved in my Father's business. I have to be . . . this is what I *must* do."

He never lost that sense of missional urgency, either!

- I *must* preach the kingdom of God *(Luke 4:43)*.
- We *must* go through Samaria *(John 4:4)*.
- The Son of Man *must* suffer *(Luke 9:22)*.
- Zaccheus, I *must* stay at your house *(Luke 19:5)*.
- I have other sheep . . . I *must* bring them also *(John 10:16)*.
- The Son of Man *must* be lifted up that whoever believes in Him will have eternal life *(John 3:14–15)*.

In a gracious but mild rebuke, Jesus responded to Mary's complaint with the subtle message, "Don't forget, Joseph isn't My father . . . God is My Father."

In Obedience

After saying all of that, you would never imagine reading this next verse in Luke's Gospel:

> ***And He went down with them and came to Nazareth, and He continued in subjection to them*** (Luke 2:51*a*).

You would expect to read, "They went down to Nazareth and they subjected *themselves* to *Him*." Or, perhaps, "And Jesus moved into the temple and became the youngest priest in the history of Israel."

No . . . none of that happened.

Jesus actually went back to Nazareth and remained under the authority of His parents. The tense of the verb indicates that Jesus continually responded to the authority of His parents.

He was still growing . . . still preparing.

By the way, knowing who He was didn't create pride or a condescending spirit toward His peasant parents. The dawning of this truth did not make Him *less* obedient to them; it profoundly *highlighted* His obedience.

The same should be true of us. Our relationship as children of God should seriously mark our relationships with humility and deference and grace.

Because the truth has dawned in our hearts that God is *our* Father by faith in His unique Son, we *must* be better spouses . . . more honest employees . . . more diligent students . . . more gracious people . . . more passionate ambassadors of the Gospel of Jesus Christ.

When young Jesus realized who He was, His obedience to His parents became even more a model for us all.

Jesus' earthly relationships were the fruit of His primary relationship to God the Father. So, also, our earthly relationships should bear the fruit of this truth dawning in our own hearts: we just so happen to have an eternal bond with *our* Father as sons and daughters. *Who we belong to should affect everything that belongs to us!*

I'm often reminded of what an older Christian leader told me one day: "The Christian life is not a lot of decisions; it's really only one. The decision is to live my life for the glory of God . . . no matter when, no matter where, no matter what."

One decision, with ongoing determination. One decision, with daily application.

Here in this first-century temple, in the life-altering scene before us, young Jesus makes a profound discovery and a godly decision: I must give My life for the glory of My Father.

And that meant, surprisingly, going back to Nazareth and remaining an obedient Child.

There wasn't anything particularly glorious about that—nothing grand or splendid, no fireworks, no claps of thunder.

It meant chores . . . homework . . . more growth spurts . . . the normal human challenges and difficulties of waiting and learning and growing.

His was a decision with ongoing determination . . . a decision for us all to make or recommit to at this very moment, whether we're six, twelve, thirty-six, eighty-six, or somewhere in between.

Here's the decision: "I will devote myself to the things of my Father; I will live to please my Father . . . no matter when, no matter where, no matter what."

Parenting the Perfect Child

Luke 2:52

If you were to comb all the biblical accounts of Christ's early life, you would discover eight different scenes that add to the drama of Jesus Christ's birth and boyhood.

Scene One

Luke 2:7–20

Angels announced His birth outdoors in a stable; shepherds were dazzled by those angels who announced the Savior's birth and went to the manger where He lay.

Scene Two

Luke 2:21

Jesus is eight days old and is identified with the covenant family of Abraham through circumcision.

Scene Three

Luke 2:22–24

Thirty days after Jesus' birth, Joseph and Mary take their Baby to the temple to present Him to God. It is in this same touching scene where Mary brings an offering characteristic of poor people: two birds offered to atone for her own uncleanness that, according to the Law, came with childbirth.

Scene Four

Matthew 2:11–12

The toddler Jesus is playing in the living room when He and His mother receive a surprise visit from wise men—kingmakers from eastern Persia; they had traveled there in anticipation of meeting the King of the Jews.

Scene Five

Matthew 2:13–15

Joseph and Mary escape to Egypt, becoming fugitives, running for their lives in the middle of the night to avoid Herod's death edict on Bethlehem boys—his attempt to kill the newborn King.

Scene Six

Matthew 2:19–23

Herod has died, and less than two years later, Joseph and Mary return with Jesus to live in Nazareth.

Scene Seven

Luke 2:41–49

Twelve-year-old Jesus is in the temple, asking and answering questions with the religious leaders. God the Father has revealed to Jesus His divine paternity—that God is, uniquely, His Father.

Scene 8

Luke 2:52

This longest scene of all will last eighteen years in Nazareth, as Jesus Christ grows from a boy to a man and, around the age of thirty, He will eventually step into the public square and announce He is more than the son of a carpenter.

As far as the record of Scripture goes, one particular verse provides a silent testimony to all that was happening in the life of Christ as He matured from a young boy into a young man. Just one verse categorically summarizes the adolescence of Jesus as He grew up in a little village called Nazareth:

> ***And Jesus kept increasing in wisdom and stature, and in favor with God and men*** (Luke 2:52).

This is very normal vocabulary, not only for the growth of God the Son but in the life of one of the great Old Testament priests by the name of Samuel. The text is similar:

> ***Now the boy Samuel was growing in stature and in favor both with the LORD and with men*** (1 Samuel 2:26).

In Luke's account of John the Baptist's growth as a little boy, he writes:

> ***And the child continued to grow and to become strong in spirit*** (Luke 1:80).

Earlier Luke had written that

> [Jesus] ***continued to grow and become strong, increasing in wisdom; and the grace of God was upon Him*** (Luke 2:40).

So by the time you arrive at this signature summary in ***Luke 2:52***, you've entered a scene which provides even more mystery than ever regarding the boyhood of Jesus.

Some would believe that Jesus had all the wisdom He needed and never increased in that attribute—or any other, for that matter.

But Luke clearly says that Jesus is advancing; He's growing in three unique ways. In fact, Luke uses three nouns to describe the growth and maturing process of Jesus: He increased in wisdom, stature, and favor.

I would agree with one New Testament scholar that these nouns convincingly argue that Jesus kept on increasing; this progress continued and there was more to follow.[1]

Frankly, we find it hard to believe that Jesus ever developed in any way . . . surely He had it all together as He slept in the manger.

If Jesus was, in fact, a sinless child—a "perfect" son—it would have meant that His development had already been perfected. But that would have violated His human nature and made of Him something less than a fully normal, growing boy, yet without sin.

The truth is it would have been possible for Jesus to do something unwise without sinning. As I stated earlier, being unwise is not the same thing as committing a sin. Aren't we glad about that?

Luke records that Jesus, 100 percent human, had to advance from immaturity to maturity . . . from silliness to sobriety . . . from naïveté to discernment . . . from uninformed actions—made through dumb, or even dangerous, decisions as young boys and girls can do—to measured and informed actions.

Jesus was not God humanized, nor was He a human deified. The mystery of the incarnation is that He, being 100 percent God, became 100 percent human, as well.

Jesus caught a cold like every child developing their immune system. His nose ran when He sneezed. He smashed His finger, had to be potty trained, and might have even been afraid of the dark.

And as He grew, He would fight temptation like any young man—yet, by virtue of the Holy Spirit's quiet supervision, Jesus would never have crossed the line into sin—not even once.

The author of Scripture didn't want us to miss this:

One who has been tempted in all things as we are, yet without sin (Hebrews 4:15).

When we believe the implications of this revelation, we discover Someone who can understand exactly how we feel.

Jesus would have scratched His knees playing with the village children just like they did; He would have burned His tongue on hot cider until He learned better; He got cold when it was cold and hot and sweaty when He played hard or worked in their simple garden or the workshop with His stepfather.

Jesus knew what it was like to be under parental authority; He was called inside to wash up just like His playmates . . .

and He would have wanted to stay out longer and play, like any child.

Jesus *knew* what it was like to be sixteen years old; He knew what it was like to be a thirty-year-old single man.

I love the inspired choice of verb for Christ's growth and development. In my text it is translated *Jesus kept increasing*. That word is *prokopto*, rendered *to advance*.[2]

The word carries the idea of *making headway or forging ahead*.[3] This verb can refer to metals being lengthened by hammering or trees being cut down in the pathway of an advancing army, making them have to literally hack their way forward.

The word needs to be understood lest we fall into the trap of believing that, for Jesus, advancement was . . . well . . . easy. When we read **Jesus kept increasing in wisdom and stature, and in favor with God and men**, we might be tempted to think, *Well, of course He did . . . what do you expect? I mean, He's deity . . . it was probably easy."*

But the opposite was true.

Because of who He was, His advancement was a billion times more difficult as a human being than any of our advancements could ever be.

Think about it: relentless concentrated attacks of demonic forces try to cause Him to sin; knowledge of His divine nature over time, as He grew, would easily wrestle with limitations of the human condition; sensitivity of His divine nature to the sinfulness of those around Him would create difficulties.

The advancement of Jesus wasn't easy. It was more like a ship making headway in a storm or a woodcutter swinging his axe until his muscles burned or a messenger determined to reach his destination against strong winds and pelting hail.

In other words, this verb *to increase* carries the idea of hard work—monotonous labor, where every step forward is a moral victory. This is exactly the nature of our own spiritual and physical advancement, isn't it?

Has progress in the Christian life ever come easy? Has obedience to God's Word been an effortless thing for you?

Do you ever feel like you're trying to walk with Christ but the headwind never stops blowing against you?

Have you ever thought about the fact that growing in grace is as slow as cutting down a forest of trees? Jesus Christ can understand our challenge. He's just like you and me: 100 percent human.

Now, for those of you who don't know me well, I'm aware that to speak of Him like this may lead you to believe I'm dishonoring the Savior.

Hardly. The trouble is we don't take the time to explore the texts related to His incarnation. But when we do, they do not cause us to denigrate the Savior—they cause us to delight in Him.

We have a Savior who understands what it means to grow in wisdom and grace against the normal resistance of the human condition with all its weaknesses.

The God Man will weep in the Garden one day with loud tears and crying *(Hebrews 5:7)*. Further, He will say:

> ***"Father! All things are possible for You; remove this cup from Me"*** (Mark 14:36).

He spoke like a man, cried like a man, and even sweat blood in utter despair and agony of spirit like a man.

But He pressed on. And His advancement has cut a path through the forest of time: ***Jesus, the author and perfecter of faith*** (Hebrews 12:2).

For every believer, Jesus Christ the Man has shown us that advancement is possible, but only as we bend our will to the will of our Heavenly Father.

We become the metal hammered by the smith; we become the axe swung by the woodsman; we become the messenger, pushing forward through inclement weather.

Frankly, the legends of church tradition can't stand the thought of Jesus facing any of this kind of trouble. Surely, Jesus and His parents had nothing but smooth sailing.

Just look at the great medieval paintings, commissioned by the Church as they pictured the virgin and her Child seated on stately thrones, upon floors of splendid mosaic patterns, under gentle canopies of blue and gold; they are clothed in rich colors and the edges of their robes are embroidered with gold.

One apocryphal writing postulates that as a young boy, Jesus assembled the boys in his village; they put their garments on the ground and He sat upon them. Then they put a crown of wreathed flowers on His head, and, like attendants waiting upon a king, they stood in order before Him on His right hand and on His left. And whoever passed that way the boys took by force, crying, "Come hither and adore the king, and then proceed upon thy way."

Nothing could be further from the truth. Nobody in the neighborhood gang was bowing before Jesus. And Joseph and Mary didn't live under canopies of blue and gold . . . their floor was dirt, not mosaic tile.

They lived in the insignificant village of Nazareth as simple, hardworking peasants with little to call their own. And when Jesus ended His ministry, He barely owned anything, either.

He was actually so normal that when He preached His first sermon at the age of thirty, everybody said, ***"Is not this the carpenter's son?"*** (Matthew 13:55). Read that, "Who does He think He is?!"

Nobody in the village rose up and said, "I knew it! I knew there was something unique about His halo . . . I knew He was God in the flesh!"

Not quite.

They were more likely to have responded, "We knew He was a responsible kid and always obedient . . . He especially seemed to love the synagogue and His studies . . . but God in the flesh? The anointed Messiah? C'mon . . . He must have hit His head with a hammer in the carpenter shop."

Jesus' life was so normal, so uneventful, so typical, so humble, and so ordinary that when He made His announcement, *no one* believed Him.

But all the while, without anyone really paying all that much attention during those eighteen years of solitude after His appearance in the temple at age twelve, Jesus evidently was making headway!

He was progressing in four different aspects that face every one of us, as well . . . every day.

Intellectual Ability

Luke refers to the first area of progression when he writes that ***Jesus kept increasing in* wisdom** (*sophia*). Sophia, for the believer, is the appropriate application of God's truth to life's circumstances; it is God's Word *demonstrated*.

So, for Christ to increase in wisdom would mean that He would need to increase in knowledge (primarily, of God's Word) and develop in His demonstration of truth.

Along the way, Jesus had to learn that $2 + 2 = 4$. He also had to learn how to read and write. Most importantly, He had to learn the sacred writings of the Old Testament.

During the days of Christ—in fact, for centuries before His birth—a Jewish child's education began in the home.

Christ's parents were His first teachers. They were to teach Jesus and the other siblings when they sat down in the house to talk or eat, when they were outside walking or working, even as they prepared to lie down, and then when they rose the next morning *(Deuteronomy 6:6–7)*. Their lives were bibliocentric. God was the center of their lives, and their conversations included Him.

Around the age of five or six, a Jewish child was sent to school: the House of the Book, so it was called. The school was attached to the local synagogue; every village had their synagogue according to the Law, and every synagogue had its school.[4] Great care was taken not to send a child to school too early, nor to overwork him when there.[5]

My school certainly didn't feel the same way!

History records for us, the school hours were fixed and attendance shortened during the summer months.[6] The teacher was often seated on a small elevation or platform, while the students sat around on the floor. This explains the concept, described in ***Acts 2:3***, that Paul was educated *at the feet* of Gamaliel.[7]

For the first five years of a child's studies, the Old Testament was their chief textbook. They would be taught to read and write their common language Aramaic but, more importantly, the language of their Law: Hebrew. It wasn't an easy language to learn.

I was at the mall some years ago with my kids, continuing our Christmas tradition of buying gifts they actually wanted, as well as choosing their own gifts for their mother that would be a surprise for her. At one point, we walked past one of those booths that are set up in the middle of the main corridor and a woman handed me a little plastic cup filled with some kind of lotion. She invited me to try it. Her accent was unusual, so I asked what her native tongue was. She responded, "It's a mixture of Russian and Hebrew." I discovered that she was a Jewess, raised in Russia, having also lived in Israel. I told her that I wished I knew my Hebrew better so that we could talk in her native tongue. Then I invited her to our church.

Imagine, someone coming to live in North Carolina by way of Russia and Israel. For the Jews living in Jesus' day, it was just as convoluted. They had lost their native tongue, having learned to speak Aramaic in Babylon where it was the official language.[8]

Their sons, primarily, had to be taught Hebrew—and for those young boys who were destined to teach the Scriptures to the next generation, they had to learn to read and write in Hebrew.

When our Lord delivered His first sermon in the synagogue of Nazareth, He first read from the Hebrew scroll of Isaiah. He had evidently learned His Hebrew lessons well.

When a five-year-old boy began his studies at the House of the Book, his very first lesson, according to their custom, was to begin working through the Book of Leviticus.[9] After that, they explored sections from the Pentateuch (the first five books of the Old Testament) and then on to the Prophets.

When I learned that Jesus as a five-year-old would have taken up His first study in the Book of Leviticus, I immediately turned to see what Christ would have first read as a little boy.

Leviticus begins with these words:

Then the LORD called to Moses and spoke to him from the tent of meeting, saying, "Speak to the sons of Israel and say to them, 'When any man of you brings an offering to the LORD, you shall bring your offering of animals from the herd or the flock. If his offering is a burnt offering from the herd, he shall offer it, a male without defect; he shall offer it at the doorway of the tent of meeting, that he may be accepted before the LORD. He shall lay his hand on the head of the burnt offering, that it may be accepted for him to make atonement on his behalf'" (Leviticus 1:1-5).

Imagine, Jesus Christ's first Hebrew lesson in school was about the unblemished sacrifice for atonement and the forgiveness of sins. Jesus, the final Sacrifice, would have read about a sacrificial system He would one day replace.

Jesus was advancing in intellectual ability as a young student.

Physical Maturity

Luke writes that ***Jesus kept increasing in wisdom and stature***. The word for stature would refer simply to age or, even, height. So He followed a normal progression and pattern in physical growth, just as He matured intellectually. Jesus went through puberty. His voice cracked, and He blushed.

Like any normal boy, He would have been mystified at the changes in His body and proud of the peach fuzz on His upper lip; maybe He flexed His muscles for His half-sisters and wrestled and raced His half-brothers. Perhaps He competed in the village games and described with excitement the fish He caught.

But growing in stature meant more than growing taller. It meant growing with regards to responsibility.

All male Jews—even the doctors of the Law—were expected to learn a trade.[10] In fact, it was required that every Jewish father teach his son what the rabbis called an "honest craft, for to fail in this is to teach him robbery, or crime."

The Apostle Paul, although preparing to become a rabbi, had also learned the craft of tentmaking—more than likely, his father's occupation.[11]

So Jesus was taught carpentry . . . this was the craft of His stepfather. Jesus learned to size up a piece of wood and to cut, shape, and craft it into something useful.

For carpenters in Nazareth, their chief task would have been to carve plows for oxen to pull, as well as yokes for their harness.

Imagine the young Man who now recognizes His relationship to God the Father . . . slip into His sandals. He knows who He is and where He's heading: ultimately the cross and then the crown, where the glory of God and the splendor of heaven await.

For eighteen years He smelled of sweat as He sawed and sanded and nailed. But no one's looking, so why not wiggle His nose or snap His fingers and *presto!* . . . a finished yoke . . . a polished table . . . a perfect plow. Imagine the business He could have cranked out for His family.

Why sweat it out?

Because He had chosen to humble Himself and become a man, accepting the limitations of mankind and working within those limitations as He labored those eighteen years in a tiny shop, taking hours to make things He could have commanded in an instant—never complaining, never saying, "Enough of this human ordeal."

There wasn't an act or miracle until His ministry began. And only then did He perform miracles for the benefit of others.

I hope you don't mind my asking the question, though: Was the Lord a *good* carpenter?

Justin Martyr, the second-century church leader in Galilee, provides the answer. He made the interesting statement that farmers were still using plows and yokes for their oxen that had been carefully crafted by Jesus Christ 75 years earlier.

Imagine that. Even though He never twitched His nose or snapped His fingers, He diligently crafted such excellent work so that long after He ascended to the Father, the farmers were still using His materials.

Jesus Christ was growing up, and the demonstration of His integrity was found in the quality of the plow He shaped with His hands.

Jesus increased in mental ability.

Jesus increased in physical maturity.

Spiritual Intimacy

Luke continues enumerating Christ's development: ***Jesus kept increasing in wisdom and stature, and* in favor with God**.

That translation can be misleading to an English reader. Cults use this verse as a proof text that, as Jesus grew up, He became more and more God's favorite—just a man who lived such an exemplary life that God decided to grant Him a favored position among men.[12]

Never mind that being the favorite of God the Father would lead Him to abandon Jesus on the cross and watch Him die a slow, tortuous death. What kind of favorite is that?

The word *favor* is *charis*, translated *grace*. The next word in the Greek New Testament is the word *para*, which means *alongside of*. We use this word for parachurch ministry. It isn't a ministry directly related to the church but, rather, a ministry *alongside* the church.

Jesus wasn't gaining grace *from* God over time. He was growing in grace *alongside of* God.

You could translate this text to read ***Jesus grew in grace by the side of God.***

In other words, the relationship between God the Son and God the Father was a growing relationship marked by grace.

Perhaps you've noticed how Jesus often pulled away from the crowd so that He could talk to His Father in private.

As Jesus grew older, His relationship with God the Father grew more important and even more intimate.

In Him we find our own desire . . . and failure. But He also models our future: perfect, sinless, unhindered fellowship with our Father—eternally unbroken, unselfish, uncluttered, unending transparent intimacy with God the Father.

There's one final aspect in which Jesus grew.

Social Integrity

Luke writes that ***Jesus kept increasing in wisdom and stature, and in favor with God and* men**.

This doesn't mean that He grew more popular with people; quite the opposite.

In fact, **Luke 4** records that most interesting moment when the Lord begins His ministry, reading from Isaiah and delivering His first sermon in His hometown synagogue of Nazareth.

The end result of His first sermon was villagers so infuriated with His announcement to ministry that they threw Him out of the synagogue and attempted to lead Him to the top of a hill where they could push Him off.

He miraculously slipped away in the commotion and thus began His public ministry.

He could have snapped His fingers and Nazareth might have exploded in a mushroom cloud.

Jesus had grown up there. He knew them and they knew Him. And they knew He'd never cheated any of them or wronged a single person . . . ever.

But now that He announces His Messianic claim, they—of all people—try to kill Him.

And He just slipped away.

What grace.

He grew in His graciousness alongside of people's offensive behavior, and He withheld His judgment while He ultimately submitted to the agony of a cross, as He died alone.

He fulfilled the very first lesson He'd learned in school: an unblemished Lamb dies to atone for the sin of the nation . . . of the world.

Frankly, I wish we had more information about the boyhood of Jesus—His life during those formative years in Nazareth. If we could have interviewed Joseph, what would you have asked him?

I would have wanted to know:
- Did you know Who He really was?
- What were the clues?
- Whenever there was an argument, did you intuitively know that Jesus was not going to be guilty of wrongdoing?
- How did you handle the other kids complaining, "How come Jesus never gets a spanking?"

I might even dare to ask Joseph if he ever scolded or spanked Jesus at any time. My best guess is that Joseph would probably hang his head and say, "Yes."

The Old Testament clearly prescribed corporal punishment. And I believe Jesus experienced discipline—not because He was imperfect, but because Joseph was imperfect.

There were times when Joseph and Mary just got it wrong.

Some time ago, my family was sitting around the dinner table, our twin sons almost 24, our daughters 22 and 16 at the time. I asked them, "When you were growing up, did I ever give you guys a spanking that you didn't deserve?" And my sons, without hesitation, said in unison, "Oh, yeah!"

Not even a moment's hesitation!

They were right . . . there were many times when I simply responded incorrectly.

I can remember as an eleven-year-old sitting in that black overstuffed chair in the living room of my boyhood home where my three brothers and I grew up. We were supposed to be doing our homework, which I normally enjoyed. *Ahem.*

Trouble was, it was a day or two before Halloween and someone at school had given us a really scary mask. That mask was the object of my attention. My mother walked by, took it away from me and put it in the closet, while she threatened, "Don't play with that again until you've finished your homework."

A few minutes later, one of my younger brothers went into the closet and got that mask out. He came up to where I was and I remember warning him, "You're gonna get in big trouble if Mom sees you with that." He laughed and kept playing around. Suddenly, we both heard Mom's footsteps on the stairway; my brother threw the mask into my lap and ran around the corner. She came down, saw the mask, yanked me up out of that chair, and before I could offer a defense, quote Scripture, or anything, she gave me one of my few undeserved spankings.

I frankly admire Joseph. I personally believe he deeply felt his own inadequacies as a father of the future Messiah.

Imagine being given the assignment of teaching the written Word to the Living Word. Imagine referring to and reading the prophecies of Scripture to a little boy who was the One of whom the prophets had spoken.

That's like God saying to me in a dream, "Stephen, I am going to give you and Marsha a son, and he will be the world's greatest scientist; he will discover mathematical and scientific formulas that will open the way for new civilizations to prosper. It's your responsibility as his father to prepare him for this life of brilliance."

I flunked Algebra. It took summer school and an academic probation as a college freshman before I finally made it through the least amount of science and math a student was required to master. The last thing I could have done is prepare a son to be a math whiz.

God effectively gave this assignment to a simple carpenter, not a rabbi; a migrant worker, not a scholar. Joseph was to teach the One who would become the world's greatest Teacher.

Why not Joseph of Arimathea? He lived during the same time. He was wealthy, had access to tutors. He was a member of the Sanhedrin, the Jewish Supreme Court. He loved the Law, he was a righteous man, and he was looking for the kingdom of God.

Did Joseph of Nazareth get mistaken for Joseph of Arimathea? Joseph of Nazareth probably wondered. And I personally believe Joseph felt what every parent often feels: someone else could do a much better job.

If you could have interviewed Mary and asked her, "Were you up to this task?" she would have responded, "Are you kidding?"

Read the biblical account carefully and you'll be reminded that the angel came to a virgin—not a saint or a princess or an experienced parent who could perfectly parent the perfect Child.

In fact, Mary's first recorded words to twelve-year-old Jesus were an ill-timed, undeserved, and unwise scolding.

And that's great news for us.

If God would choose those two people to parent the Messiah, God can use us, too.

What kind of people does God choose to raise a generation of Christ followers . . . to serve as His ambassadors before a desperately needy world?

Let me *paraphrase* the Apostle Paul's answer to that question:

> ***Consider your calling . . . consider the place where God has appointed you . . . God didn't choose among the brilliant . . . not many with noble upbringing . . . not many with powerful connections . . . He has chosen the ordinary students to teach the brilliant; He has chosen the weak and insignificant people in the eyes of the world to radically impact those who seem to be on top of it all*** (1 Corinthians 1:25-26).

Mary and Joseph were not ready to parent the perfect Child. But they were obedient.

The songwriter captures the mystery of parenting the Messiah with a series of insightful questions:

> *Mary, did you know that your baby Boy*
> *Will one day walk on water?*
> *Mary, did you know that your baby Boy*
> *Will save our sons and daughters?*
>
> *Did you know that your baby Boy*
> *Has come to make you new?*
> *This child that you've delivered*
> *Will soon deliver you.*
>
> *Mary, did you know that your baby Boy*
> *Will give sight to a blind man?*
> *Mary, did you know that your baby Boy*
> *Will calm a storm with His hand?*
>
> *Did you know that your baby Boy*
> *Has walked where angels trod?*
> *And when you kiss your little Baby,*
> *You have kissed the face of God?*
> *Mary, did you know?*
>
> *The blind will see, the deaf will hear;*
> *The dead will live again!*
> *The lame will leap, the dumb will speak*
> *The praises of the Lamb!*
>
> *Mary, did you know that your baby Boy*

Is Lord of all creation?
Mary, did you know that your baby Boy,
Will one day rule the nations?

Did you know that your baby Boy
Is heaven's perfect Lamb?
This sleeping Child you're holding
Is the Great I AM![13]

Having studied carefully the boyhood of Jesus, I can say with some certainty that Mary *didn't* know . . . at least, not fully. Joseph didn't fully know, either. The boyhood of Jesus would be a mystery to them both.

Apart from the Holy Spirit who dwells within us, we all are unlikely candidates to accomplish whatever it is that God has appointed us to do.

And of all the things we might want to accomplish, these four advancements from Luke's profound text would be a terrific place to focus more attention and energy and prayer:

1. That we might also **develop in our understanding** and application of God's Word;

2. That we might also grow up to **accept the responsibilities** of wherever God has placed us;

3. That we might also **walk alongside of God** our Father;

4. That we might also **demonstrate grace and integrity** to those who live around us . . . regardless of how they act.

May the boyhood of Jesus provide the benchmarks of personal growth in our own lives as we also grow in the knowledge and grace of our Lord Jesus Christ.

Endnotes

CHAPTER 1

[1] Adapted from M. R. James, *The Apocryphal Infancy Gospel of Thomas: Translation and Notes* (Oxford, Clarendon Press, 1924).

[2] J. Dwight Pentecost, *The Words and Works of Jesus Christ* (Zondervan, 1981), 62.

[3] G. Campbell Morgan, *The Gospel According to Luke* (Fleming H. Revell, 1931), 40.

[4] John MacArthur, sermon manuscript, *http://w.w.gty.org/Resources/Sermons/42-28*.

[5] William Barclay, *The Gospel of Luke* (Westminster Press, 1975), 24.

[6] Pentecost, 65.

[7] J. Reiling & J. L. Swellengrebel, *A Translator's Handbook on the Gospel of Luke* (United Bible Society, 1971), 128.

[8] John Phillips, *Exploring the Gospel of Luke* (Kregel, 2005), 78.

[9] Edited from R. Kent Hughes, *Luke: Volume 1* (Crossway, 1998), 95.

[10] Phil Cross, "Grace Has a Face" (Cameron Hill Music, 2001).

CHAPTER 2

[1] Quotes taken from James Montgomery Boice: *Nehemiah, Learning to Lead* (Revell Company, 1990) & "Churchill, Sir Winston Leonard Spencer," *Microsoft (R) Encarta Encyclopedia* (Funk & Wagnalls, 1994).

[2] John MacArthur, *Matthew: Volume 1* (Moody Press, 1985), 29.

[3] W. E. Vine, *Vine's Expository Dictionary of Old and New Testament Words* (Thomas Nelson, 1997), 180.

[4] James Montgomery Boice, *Matthew: Volume 1* (Baker, 2001), 31.

[5] Ibid, 32.

[6] John Phillips, *Exploring the Gospels: Matthew* (Loizeaux, 1999), 44.

[7] Ibid, 40.

[8] R.C.H. Lenski, *The Interpretation of St. Matthew's Gospel* (Augsburg Publishing, 1964), 80.

[9] Ritz Rienecker/Cleon Rogers, *Linguistic Key to the Greek New Testament* (Regency, 1976), 4.

[10] MacArthur, 40.

[11] Edited from William Barclay, *The Gospel of Matthew: Volume 1* (Westminster Press, 1975), 35.

[12] Rienecker/Rogers, 222.

[13] Phillips, 46.

[14] MacArthur, p. 45.

[15] Bruce Larson, *The Communicator's Commentary* (Word Books, 1983), 59.

CHAPTER 3

[1] Adapted from Warren W. Wiersbe, *Be Compassionate: Luke 1–13* (Victor Books, 1989), 32.

[2] William Barclay, *The Gospel of Luke* (Westminster Press, 1975), 29.

[3] R. Kent Hughes, *Luke: Volume 1* (Crossway, 1998), 99.

[4] Hughes, 100.

[5] Ibid.

[6] R.C.H. Lenski, *The Interpretation of Luke's Gospel* (Augsburg Publishing, 1946), 162.

[7] "Mother Forgets Child at 6th Birthday Party," CBS4.com (6-05-06).

[8] G. Campbell Morgan, *The Gospel According to Luke* (Fleming H. Revell Company, 1931), 44.

[9] Barclay, 29.

[10] J. Reiling & J.L. Swellengrebel, *A Translator's Handbook on the Gospel of Luke* (United Bible Society, 1971), 151.

[11] Ibid, 152.

[12] Ivor Powell, *Luke's Thrilling Gospel* (Kregel Publications, 1965), 79.

[13] Lenski, 167.

[14] J. Dwight Pentecost, *The Words and Works of Jesus Christ*, (Zondervan, 1981), 76.

[15] E. Michael & Sharon Rusten, *The One Year Christian History* (Tyndale, 2003), 680.

CHAPTER 4

[1] R.C.H. Lenski, *The Interpretation of St. Luke's Gospel* (Augsburg Publishing House, 1946), 170.

[2] Fritz Rienecker/Cleon Rogers, *Linguistic Key to the Greek New Testament* (Regency, 1976), 145.

[3] Gerhard Kittel, editor, *Theological Dictionary of the New Testament, Abridged in One Volume* (Eerdmans, 1985), 939.

[4] David Smith, *The Days of His Flesh: The Earthly Life of Our Lord and Savior Jesus Christ* (Harper & Brothers, 1913), 20.

[5] Alfred Edersheim, *The Life and Times of Jesus the Messiah* (Eerdmans, 1967), 232.

[6] Ibid.

[7] Smith, 20.

[8] Everett F. Harrison, *A Short Life of Christ* (Eerdmans, 1975), 59.

[9] Edersheim, 232.

[10] Donald Guthrie, *Jesus the Messiah* (Zondervan, 1972), 34.

[11] Smith, 21.

[12] G. Campbell Morgan, *The Gospel According to Luke* (Fleming H. Revell, 1931), 46.

[13] Mark Lowry & Buddy Greene, "Mary, Did You Know?" (Word Music, LLC, 1991).

Scripture Index

Reference	Page
Genesis 17	11
Exodus 13:21	31
Exodus 24:17	31
Leviticus 1:1–5	84
Leviticus 12	17
Numbers 18	18
Numbers 24:17	31
Deuteronomy 6:6–7	82
1 Samuel 2:26	74
Psalms 113–118	54
Hosea 11:1	44
Matthew 1:20	64
Matthew 1:21	14
Matthew 2	29
Matthew 2:2	30
Matthew 2:5	31
Matthew 2:9*b*	33
Matthew 2:11	32
Matthew 2:11*b*	33
Matthew 2:11–12	72
Matthew 2:12	34
Matthew 2:13	37/39
Matthew 2:13–15	72
Matthew 2:14	38
Matthew 2:15	46
Matthew 2:16–18	45

Reference	Page
Matthew 2:18	46
Matthew 2:19–20	47
Matthew 2:19–23	73
Matthew 2:20*b*–21	47
Matthew 2:22	48
Matthew 2:23	48
Matthew 5:17	9
Matthew 13:55	80
Matthew 16:18 KJV	28
Mark 3:21	65
Mark 14:36	79
Luke 1:31	14
Luke 1:47	21
Luke 1:80	74
Luke 2	21
Luke 2:7–20	71
Luke 2:9	31
Luke 2:20	5
Luke 2:21	10/14/71
Luke 2:22	17
Luke 2:22*b*	19
Luke 2:22–24	72
Luke 2:23	17
Luke 2:25	23
Luke 2:26	23
Luke 2:28*b*	24

Reference	Page
Luke 2:29–32	24
Luke 2:40	74
Luke 2:41	51
Luke 2:41–49	73
Luke 2:43*a*	55
Luke 2: 43*b*–44*a*	55
Luke 2:45–46*a*	57
Luke 2:46*b*–47	60
Luke 2:49	62
Luke 2:50	63
Luke 2:51*a*	67
Luke 2:52	71/73/74
Luke 4	89
Luke 4:43	67
Luke 9:22	67
Luke 19:5	67
John 1:12*a*	20
John 2:11	42
John 3:14–15	67
John 4:4	67
John 8:12	25
John 8:41	12
John 10:16	67
Acts 2:3	82
1 Corinthians 1:25–26	93
Philippians 2:6	59
Philippians 2:7	59
Hebrews 3	44
Hebrews 4:15	57/76
Hebrews 5:7	79
Hebrews 5:8	29
Hebrews 7:26	57
Hebrews 9:14	9
Hebrews 12:2	79
1 Peter 2:22	57
1 John 2:2	9
1 John 3:5	57
Revelation 22:16	31

Other Books by Stephen Davey

Esther Commentary

Scandals abound in a drama cast in the ancient Persian Empire. In the midst of political intrigue and betrayal, a beautiful orphan girl suddenly becomes the leading character, as God's providence rescues His people from certain death. At first glance, Esther is the heroine and Mordecai the master manipulator. Take a closer look, however, and you'll discover that behind the scenes, God is pulling the strings as His sovereign providence unfolds.

Nehemiah Commentary

As you dust off the memoirs of this ordinary man, Nehemiah, you will likely be inspired to serve the faithful God whom Nehemiah followed: the One who led His obedient servant to attempt impossible, extraordinary things for His glory. Join Stephen in this study as he encourages you to make a stand for Christ . . . even when you stand alone.

The Myths, Messangers, and Mystery of Christmas

Because of the watered down, trivialized holiday season, the Church is in danger of forgetting the true significance of Christmas. People have forgotten that the Christmas story is actually a brutal scene: a lonely, desperate set of circumstances that takes the reader on an emotional roller coaster. The story begins with intrigue and ends with murder. Experience anew the real meaning of Christmas in Stephen's three message series, The Myths, Messengers and Mystery of Christmas.

For more books by Stephen Davey or to order go to:
www.wisdomonline.org

SHEPHERDS
THEOLOGICAL SEMINARY

There is an undeniable privilege of learning how to be a shepherd from someone who wears the fragrance of sheep—someone who knows how to use a shepherd's staff. In fact, there's nothing quite like a professor with a few splinters in his hands—a teacher who knows the pain and pleasure of serving the Lord in the pastureland of ministry. At Shepherds Theological Seminary, students will learn from those who practice on Sunday what they teach on Monday.

Degrees Offered

Master of Divinity
Master of Arts in Church Ministry
Bachelor of Theology
Associate of Church Ministry
Certificate of Graduate Studies

Shepherds Theological Seminary, fully accredited by Transnational Association of Christian Colleges and Schools [TRACS], is currently housed on the beautiful campus of Colonial Baptist Church in Cary, North Carolina, a short driving distance from Raleigh, Chapel Hill, and Durham.

www.shepherds.edu
(800) 672-3060